Flesh-Toned Redemption

Poems by Cydnie Odessa

Printed in the United States of America
Essyntial Life Press, 2014

ISBN 978-0-9907684-0-1

THIS BOOK
IS DEDICATED TO

Those that came before me and set up legacy: Mavis Swire: Saint, Aunt Dorothy: Supporter Supreme, Grandma Ada Marie: the Quilter, Theobald Wilson: the Photographer, Opalanga Pugh: the Storyteller, "Nani" Odessa: The Lover, Nana: The Fighter, Grandma Nikki: the Historian.

All Johnson Cousins near and far.

All of my friends on their own distinct journey who have ever walked with me—Aaron B., Joy R., Traci C., E. Jo, C. Mo., Lisa H., I love you.

My GE's and my NCA&T "Aggies."

All Sinners & Saints like me.

Everyone who listens to AM 670 KLTT, AM 810 KLVZ, or 1220 AM KLDC. Anyone who has ever listened to "Broken and Beautiful with the REAL Traci Rock."

Every "Fellow Employee" I've ever had. Every "ex-schoolmate," and all my "Friends" on FB.

"Do not conform any longer to the pattern of this world, but be transformed by the renewing of your mind. Then you will be able to test and approve what God's will is—his good, pleasing, and perfect will."

—Romans 12:2

ACKNOWLEDGEMENTS

To my Lord and Savior, Jesus Christ, for all the inspiration, through the good and bad, because You have ultimately deemed it for my good.

My Mother, Claudia-Marie Wilson, for listening and helping me "type it out."

My Father, Sid Wilson, for all those early years of "journaling" you made me do, and for always believing that "I could." Thanks for being my #1 Fan.

My brother, Theo, your life is an inspiration to me, too. Thanks for all your moral support.

To the Van Norton's, my moral support, and inspirations.

To my talented "Roundtable" of friends and mentors: Rachel M., Shaunya B., Cassia H., Traci R., Kim T., Tessa F., Darren R. You all never cease to inspire me. All of your input has been "duly noted!"

Letora Fortune Anderson, my Illustrator, your art is truly anointed.

To all the Poets of Denver, voices of our generation. To Café Nuba, To Freedom of Speech and The Speakout, where I began to find my voice.

To Mrs. Pensal McCray and all my former teachers, professors who told me to keep writing, and Shel Silverstein, my favorite poet, thank you.

FREEDOM (A FOREWORD)

That moment when you recognize
that God is BRINGING YOU BACK
to that ONE DESIRE you always had.
That "Inner Child" that IS you.
The one, secure in her artistry,
knows that no one BUT GOD
is the boss of me!
With her EVERY living being, her life means
EVERYTHING!
Livelihood in Christ—That's King!
Though God be her "Superior" she WILL NOT
remain "inferior" to the PLANS He has for her!
For she IS THAT CHILD!
WILD at heart for PERFORMING ART.
FULL of Rainbows,
floating,
on the Hope that IS to come!
She has simply been asleep.
Possibly comatose.
However now, she is WIDE AWAKE,
ready to take claim of what has ALWAYS been
rightfully hers.
Her words, her spirit.
She KNEW INNATELY IN!!!
Her love for people,
her hope in their dreams!
Her desire to inspire with her every living being!
She, knows that:
No, you can't "SHUT ME UP" with
FEAR
and depravity because
I have not. Lost.
Anything.

PREFACE

It was not until now that I could publish this work. Now is the time. It would not have made sense to BE what it IS until NOW. This work is my first collection of poetry—over a decade in the making, a compilation of my personal life experiences written from places of raw emotion and heart-felt grievances of my own psyche. Be that as it may, "Flesh-Toned Redemption" is literally, a journey. What I mean by calling it a "journey" is that it "highlights" my explorations and viewpoints of sexuality, race and ethnicity, and overall identity as it pertains to actually being a woman of the 21st Century. It also then begins to illuminate the journey into Spiritual Healing.

It is important to note the timeline in which this poetry was written. One of these poems originated when I was in adolescence (I'll leave THAT to your discernment), and many of them have sprung from my experiences in my "college days." Many of which, define me as an "Educated Black Woman" living in "White America," just to put it plainly. This "Black Experience" has played a major role in my search for "Identity" over the years of my life's journey. You will see the roles of "Race" and "ethnicity" play out distinctly in the words of much of my poetry, and I could not have left any of them out. Like it or not, my "Race" has played an integral role in making me into the woman that I am today.

The woman that I am today...who is that, you ask? Well, I honestly would need to hand all credit back to my Creator, my Lord and Savior, Jesus Christ. People may simply not be interested in that last sentence, but it is the truth of who I am today. I became "Born Again" in 2010. With that journey came the truth of my calling, which is to bring the "word of my testimony" to the forefront, and in this is my flesh, my life in blood, sweat, tears, and heartbreak; a testament to the darkness in us all. It is the angst of being "a part" of humanity. The suffering that comes from being classified "different" from the status quo, and the New Life and strength being found in the "Identity of Christ."

INTRODUCTION

"Flesh-Toned Redemption" is a work that I now consider to be an "Old Testament" of my life. It is set to be a "past-tense" introduction to my "journey of womanhood" in post-modern America. Having said that, each work will speak for itself. I will also say here, that since I have been "renewed in mind, heart, and soul," I have "dampened out" all "curse words" with their proper, modern "substitutes," because I am choosing not to "taint" my lips in their re-reading of my work. You will notice that the Contents of "Flesh-toned Redemption" are divided into three sections: FLESH, TONES, and REDEMPTION. Each section serves as a "marker" for the type of content therein.

I begin with the FLESH section, as a statement of "beginnings." The FLESH is also very vulnerable, very gritty, and poignant. This section explores the theme of sexual exploration, and its potential consequences, to the fullest. The poems within this section include the likes of: "To Be A Virgin", as I began this journey (and wrote this poem) as a virgin, and was a virgin long after many of my peers had taken the plunge into the "sex life." "Zombie Pt. I" explores the realm of "toxic relationships," while, "Your (S)Expiration" gives way to us stopping and thinking about what we're all "doing it" for. The rest is history that you would be sorry NOT to re-read.

The TONES section makes for the BULK of this collection. Within TONES lies a piece of my identity as a middle-class, African-American woman as well as a post-modern, college-educated liberal (at the time). It's me being young, gifted and Black, waking up to the world around me, and coming into the light that through it all, I am finding myself "The Essyntial" (my former stage name). I am a woman of MANY "tones," as you soon will see. "Nigger-Free (A Liberation Rant)" will definitely be an "eyebrow-raiser" for some. It is how I personally see the word, have seen the word, and have determined its use for myself. Let me be clear: It's a very NEGATIVE term, a CURSE word, and I will clarify here, that it should only be seen and used (if it must be used) to CURSE. Therefore, it belongs with all the rest of our "foul" idioms in the English language, and banned from casual conversation as such, unless one intends to be specifically, and intentionally vulgar. "I Will Grow My Naps" is every "Natural's" anthem, and a testament to my personal "Black Hair Evolution/Revolution."

Last but not least, we have REDEMPTION. I am coming into a "completely new" understanding of who I am and who I am not. There's healing, and much purpose here. Kicking off with "The Breakthrough," being haunted by my "My Zombie" and then dealing with my "So Called Adversity," I'm beginning to see things differently. I'm "Armed For Love" and ready to serve you "My Reality Check." "Love Citadel" will stand alone, and I know I am up for criticism, but all I'll be able to say is, "Aren't You Glad" you've read it all?

CONTENTS

FLESH

TONES

REDEMPTION

FLESH

TO BE A VIRGIN

To be a virgin
Means never having had your soul
tied and bound to another man by
way of your womb, which harnesses
the child he's never going to father.
To be a virgin,
Means freedom of mental from the treacherous
dread of steal tongs that force their way down...
pushing...gliding...sliding like the
iron wheels inside the tracks of the Lightrail
up against the walls of your CERVIX, pressing hard
and diving deep as the Navy Seals on a submarine
to Australia!
Pressing hard as if the JAWS OF LIFE
Weren't enough to get you open for your annual pap smear...
To be a virgin...
To be a VIRGIN
Means less worries about what the Gyno
Found on their visit to your DOWNTOWN area...hm,
AND not having to give 'giving blood' a second thought.
To be a virgin...
To be a VIRGIN @ 21...hm, imagine that.
Well, I don't have to.
Have to EVER worry about whether or not I am
The school yard "JUMP OFF"
And when the male sex looks my way,
They haven't a word to say but "Hey, how are you today?"
And I can speak and say "I'm Fine."
When in my mind I know that I AM FYYYYNE!
Like a wine...only getting better with time,
Only ever freer in my mind, knowing
This in THIS life, MY BODY HAS ONLY BEEN MINE.
And in knowing this, I know myself to be a gift.

To be a virgin. Not so bad.
To be a virgin. Never sad.
Never sad about giving away the only thing
that really mattered...that HE has now had.
Never in compromise of my emotions, character,
Or being.
To be a virgin,
is looking within the pages of a book, and
not just at its cover...

TO BE A VIR-GIN
Is redefining the meaning of the word, "LOVER"
For I too am a lover... sharing with the world a love for myself,
before any other.

STANDARDZ

When it comes to men, I've come to realize that
My standards are high
Although not to the degree that you fancy
Not status wise, or even *phallus* size
epitomize the reasons why
I realize my standards are high…

High—although not sky, each year they rise
And I become more & more wise…
For most of these GUYS fail to recognize

things inside of them
that they kill-off in spite of them
That could have been of insight to them
Could have enlightened them to become more than one
    MIGHT have been…

But NO, instead they welcome the PLIGHT of themselves.

And if they were kings,
No one could tell.

Not even by the way they carry themselves
BURY themselves, under these loathsome shells
Of un-integrity.

But baby, if you got it, let me see!
Because it's not WHAT you're wearin' so much
As HOW you're wearin' it that matters to me.

Whether it's the newest from Sean John, white or black tee,
PROJECT to me the powers that be!

Hold your head high, don't cover up eyes,

Walk like you SEE!

Standards such as these apply to me I'd like to
See them rise to these!

I need a man who is who he is
And NOT who he see's!
One who can see further than where he is.
His hometown does not dictate to him who he is…
Who can envision a thousand more lives than the
one that he lives.
Who receives with all pleasure
And appeases me all the more pleasingly when he gives

Lives life to the fullest within his means
Takes time to share with others in his dreams
One who challenges my intellects and fertilizes my being.

Thinks outside of himself and searches for further
    teachings…
Someone who knows the PURPOSE to his being.

Standards such as these apply to thee,
I'd like to see them RISE to these…
STANDARDS I realize, for right now,
are <u>too high</u>
to be.

UR (S)EXPIRATION

A being has a body has a sexpiration date.
A being has a body has an expiration date.
What to it can u rate?
This entity, not invincible
This entity, behold me,
Quite expendable
So then I ask myself,
Is it sensible?

Is it sensible?
To "up the ante" on my expiration date??
Within wakes of bounteous sexual exploration
How can this body of mine ever be so safe from
Early expiration…?
To my DIS-elation it is easy to say….
'Tis far better to wait!
Ease up on the sex plate.
'Cause the more bounteous the platter,
the greater consequence is the matter.
The price, all too great for this…temporary
Stimulation
Titillation, far more than
Masturbation: Copulation is the term—
MOST do.
Body delicate, body bold, body brilliant.
Body brittle.
But yet—penis & vagina remain the inexorable centerfold…

So much
comes from
organs,
so little.

MAKE BELIEVE

Let's pretend.
I want to pretend that you & I
Made love with protection until we got off,
And got hungry.
Showered, dressed, and went for breakfast

Pretend the "unspeakable" didn't come, see…
Pretend that condom *wasn't still in me*…
You think it's funny now?
Well come, laugh at me—crashing at this party
See 'cause, in the back of my mind,
I'm NOT pregnant…
Pretend that this shot of vodka won't kill a seed
There is NO SEED
WE'RE JUST MAKE BELIEVE
It wasn't MAKE BELIEVE when I took that
PLAN B…
No not make believe when I hit the floor,
Head sore
Heart SO HARD…
Think I may be pregnant? Well, let me see…
What can I do to justify ME???
Hm, let's think,
Because it was MY CHOICE to let YOU *DEFILE* ME
with "Twisted Pleasures" brand,
to boot!
Nonetheless, what was done is done
We prayed before I took the pill.

ZOMBIE PT. I

And they,
tear into your flesh like they were zombies...
She had a zombie,
If only she could see
But instead she chose to stick around and beat a deadbeat.
It's not funny.
She really had a stick—long, uncut, and hard like her favorite
    part of him.
And she was whoopin' him with all that she had...
Thinkin' about how all these men
would never be dad.
It's sad,
how she couldn't walk away.
She chose to stay and beat a dead man down—
Stiletto heal crushing his heart into the ground.
He was a dead weight—flat, cold, heavy and
the fight was epic.
Multiple thrusts with her mighty stick
speared into his ribcage.
He snatches it out, tosses it aside,
Spits blood at her feet
And barks,
"Yea, EFF you, babe!"

With that, he lunges at her and
Gnashes a chunk right from her neck.
She screams—agony & ecstasy
All shades of gray in her mind,
As once and for all time,
she remains a slave—she
now a zombie.
She
Couldn't see the wrong—she

couldn't feel the weight
of a deadbeat in time. She
forever blind.
He
did engulf her flesh, he
ate up all her best parts
Them,
now a couple
of dead hearts.
Dead hearts unfulfilled.

Deathly
Enthralled in
Ample insecurity &
Desolation
Heavily
Empty with
Apathetic
Rear-view inquiries
Tumultuously seeking more time.

THAT THING

I get home.
No matter my prior whereabouts…
There she sits like the gateway that holds all the answers to my
   prayers
Quietly waiting for me to open her,
Like a Pandora's box of ceaseless wonders.
Waiting, her entity calls to me
Beckoning that I come and unlatch her top.
Her glorious light beaming ever so coyly,
Drawing me nearer, waiting to enthrall me in
Her seemingly endless illumination….

Da hell you think this is!? I'm jus talking bout my Laptop!
Better yet, my MAC BOOK PRO! It is a beautiful instrument…
Hehe, and we've only JUST begun…
See, my Mac book pro is JUST the tool.
What's inside…let's face it…
SHE'S GOT EVERYTHING!
Everything PLUS one thing…
Lately that one thing…
It encapsulates everything else, sometimes I wonder if
My Mac book is jealous, see
(Sing)"It's that ONE THING that got me trippin"
Like…it's the tree of knowledge,
in my Garden of Eden.
Tempting me ever….so…much….more…all….the….time.
To know.
I MUST know…I must know….SO MUCH!
Like a vortex, it draws me in—magnetically,
It seems to rearrange ALL MY PRIORITIES—-
More often than not,
Reducing them, from incomplete—to nothing.
This one thing, oh no! Here it comes…!

FACEBOOOOOOOK!!!
I get home.
And the only thing I do first,
Is take time to be alone.
Then I unlatch my Mac book,
and me and Facebook begin to bone!
My mind is thoroughly lubricated,
Soon to be wasted neurons salivating
For all the useless information I then begin to
take in.
Though useless, it feels so goood!
mmmm…me and Facebook bonded now,
sharing simultaneous intimate connections that
make me sometimes suck on
my fingers…ooh, Facebook!
Ow! Facebook!
Uh huh! Facebook!
Ohh Facebook! Don't stop now! FACEBOOK!!
Ahahaha! Facebook!
I COULD GO FOR HOURS ON FACEBOOK!!!
Umhm…
Sometimes I like to share my thoughts with it—
And dig this!
All my "friends" are already there…
And they ALL like to SHARE…!
Some of 'em put up videos…
And we all share photos…we even 'TAG'
each other…
And some even "tweet" their facebooks…
while others share notes…of prose or poetry
of lessons learned…and those who
oppose are free to 'comment' openly…
They can 'like' me…
And I ALWAYS hope…they…do.
Huh, me and Facebook,

What
An
Ego
We create.
Uh! Wait a minute!
Why did he say that...on HER page!?
Ooh! What did she say on his!?
Well! That was ONLY 4 hours ago!! (gasp)
WAIT 'til I see him again...
O-M-G! I LOVE that song!
Ugh! What's WRONG with them??
How could they NOT love it!?
UGH!!! LOOK at the way she spelled that!
S-M-H...Idiot!
When's she going to put my pictures up!?
I CAN'T BELIEVE she put THAT picture up!!
Oh! Someone wrote on my wall...
Do I even KNOW them??
L-O-L...Oh facebook...I love that picture of me...
Oh facebook—that one, too! Oh, facebook...
Wow, how did they know I would like a
Christian man...?
They know how many friends we share...
They know who our relatives are...
They know what our favorite colors are...
They know our names, faces, and ages.
They know where we work!
Oh Facebook...
You're like the man who grew on me.
The man I 'never knew' I always wanted...
And oh how we've bonded!
And you have met all my friends and family...
And now I see you,
And share myself with you
morning...noon...and night.

We're addicted to each other, now.
For you, and you alone,
I stifle my other priorities.
Because we're connected now,
there's no way out.
6 years strong, you and me.
I'm down for you…
Until you start chargin "small fees"!

Hey, they say the first step is admitting
you have a problem…well there you have it.

CONFESSIONS OF A FACEBOOK JUNKIE!
Volume I. LOL..!
Oh…That reminds me!
I gotta go update my status!
Gotta keep it current! Keep it current to life! Keep it
current to life! To life! To life! To life! OH Facebook!
GIVE ME BACK MY LIFE!!!!

NIGGER-FREE (A LIBERATION RANT)

The last time that white man said that he hated
hip hop to me, never for a good reason,
Just hated it. That did it!
I slid my way past to get to the sink
loose lips I had, and out did it sink:
"YOU'RE SUCH A NIGGER."
His blue eyes widened, astonished.
Razor lips quiver in utter disbelief.
I said "Oh you thought that word was
reserved just for me!?
te-hee-hee-hee
"But I'm" he said
And before he continued
"A Nigger!!!" I said.
Now to all my 'NIGGAS' out there who
would simply disagree,
Look it up in today's Webster
and you will see, a "NIGGER"
is someone who speaks
ignorantly. One, a person who is
ignorant, indignant an Effing
degenerate not worthy of me, my
time or precious energy!
So now we all know, the world
is FULL OF NIGGERS! See?!

Now NIGGA versus NIGGER,
the supposed controversy....
NIGGA is ignorant of the word
NIGGER thus making it into a
NIGGER. But a NIGGER disguised
as a NIGGA jus' makes
that damn NIGGER word bigger!

Then we have a bunch of "ignorants"
aka Niggers runnin' around thinkin'
that they're NIGGAS.
But a NIGGA'S a positive thing! (oh!)
Cuz we erased (er) and made it OUR
name. But the problem with ER is the
world never got the (ah) memo and
to the masses (not "massa's") to the
MASSES the words are still one
and the same And it comes with
historical shame.
The history
Our history
Their history
Our misery
These Niggers uttered it to us in hate!
Threw it at us, that word, and made it
OUR NAME!
We turned it around, changed the game
that misery word from history, took it
back, placed our claim—
 but NIGGAS CAN NEVER BE
NIGGERS OF
HISTORY!
Cuz if we forget the legacy of bigotry
someone else can use it to create
some more NIGGERY!
And, all this argument, the
controversy of it, boils inside of me!
The endless NIGGER word controversy
it's liberating me!
It's liberating me!
In such a way that I accept the word for
the true definition, and it's something
everyone can be!

And if the blind don't
quit leading the blind...how else could
they see?
So shamelessly, I'll proclaim this,
and be free:
The world is full of NIGGERS.
That could mean you, and sometimes...
me.
White people can be real niggers,
but not exclusively.
Black people know a
nigger when they meet one.
And now that we know this, we can be
NIGGER-FREE.

And my people, the next time a white
person say somethin' ignorant and
otherwise to you,

You can reply:
"NIGGER PLEASE!"

AFTER NIKKI MINAJ & RHIANNA

We are a society suffering
From mutations—emulations
mutants making money off of new generations.

What's NEXT?
I'm afraid to see.
Because any further gone
And we won't remember the importance
of being free.
We're just degenerative recycled images
of the same exact thing!
"Sluts" in spandex and stilettos!
Self-centered fantasies
Parading
In that good ol' "green!" Money.
Fans have got to feed their idols and their idols have to be…
Pretty. Perfect, and irrevocably
damaged.

A reflection of what we all want to be.
Untouchable.
Unattainable.
Unreachable. BUT
Unashamedly BROKEN!
We love that story!
Can't get enough—we are all
Dirty. Pretty things.
And today's poppy charting "Artists"
They do it PERFECT!
Now we can ALL be FAME MONSTERS
It's the new case of "commonplace."
'Cause we're all striving to be
PERFECTLY DAMAGED

& making good off of our ASSETS
you see, it's easy
once you take your clothes off...
and you're pretty.
The 5 senses were not created equal!
People tend to see more
And listen less
And the sex, the sex, the sex—
Hey, who can resist?? Ya know what I mean??
And the SEX never fails to captivate
A society.
We are vexed.
And doomed.
Far too consumed with it all.

FOR OUR SKIN

This skin
My skin
My brown skin holds me
in.
Keeps me together
encases my truth.
My skin,
Brown from my youth.
I knew,
It told me I was Black.
This skin
in my history
was a sin.
Sin to be Black.
The mark of sin,
Black skin.
It was *Them*,
The ones with that 'other' skin,
who had my spirit condemned.
My body image broken,
and now I'm *chokin'*
on my own existence…
And now, I *hate* myself.
Their own image
subjected upon me.

Now, I am too ugly
To comprehend my own
reflection.
My skin.
A constant subject of
'stipulation' to them.
My skin.

Black, bleached, burnt, bruised,
Soaked, strangled, wrangled, whipped,
Scalped, lynched, pinched, prodded,
Branded, broken, *bought* and *sold*...
My skin, so...wrong...?
My skin,
Strong.
Stronger than a mother who
smothers her baby...
to save it from the evil of
chattel slavery.
Stronger than—
7...point...scale
Earthquakes.
My skin,
the color of mud.
Baked in the sun to
match the deeper hues
of the earths fine crust...
My skin, secretly,
It infuses *their* lust!
My skin,
It has endured much.
Our skin.
A testament to all phases of humanity:
Pain, grief, passion, love,
courage, hope & faith...
Our skin,
The color of our leaders,
who now run the country.
Our skin,
Always breaking barriers...
Our skin,
Bringing those that sin to justice.
Our skin,

From black, to blue, to white....
and all hues in between,
Let (finally) freedom reign supreme,
For now, more than ever before...
I reflect an American Dream.

TONES

SHE

Look at her.
Who she be?
Who are we?
What makes HER, She?
I heard she's this.
Well I bet she's that.
Well I know this...
Where SHE stay at?
Well, I know she come around when...
Look at her, what she know?
I think she thinks she...?
Well, I heard...

She walks on steadfast running shoes,
Running on upward, to the pathways, headed towards flight.
On her back, she carries the roadmaps,
In her heart, she carries the light.
The light, given to her by ancestral spirits
of the deep-rooted past,
Kindled by the torch that was handed into her
grasp.
The torch will be passed, not by hand,
but by blood.
The blood that will one day be a product of
her, and her future love.
Who She be?
SHE is bearer of wood & bamboo sticks, bricks
And whatever else is needed.
Building bridges to what's to come.
What is to come of her people if she does
not make it strong, filling the gaps and cricks.
SHE is connecting what was once lost to what
SHE is soon destined to find.

Not wanting to leave any other of the
ancestral values behind.
She knows this.
She knows this because she knows that
Nothing else shall be erased & forgotten,
Still, SHE must take everything in stride.

SHE is Queen mother of the eastern worlds and all of
Humanity.
She is the one who holds the key.
But still, who SHE be?
She is hungry, NO—more like starved.
Starved of the hidden knowledge she longs to
Find but cannot yet begin to seek.
Starved of he TRUTH that her ancestry bleeds
Hungry for a life that she cannot lead.
Hungry for the path of truth that will not mislead her.
Hungry for the "self" in her that longs to be her.
Longs to be heard…
Hungry for the earth-shaking awakening through
Truth that will bring about great change.
Rearrange the game.
Give freedom its REAL name.
All she really wants is change through truth,
truth through change.
SHE does not want to be the one to blame.
SHE is the one who carries the light,
Will bring light, store light & distribute IT to the next 'They'.
In time, all will know SHE.
She, who is brown on the surface,
With many things from within,
But no one knows what's beyond the flesh,
What lies beneath her skin.
For within her is a lantern passed from generations
That have already been.

But no one knows the desolate-dank
That seeps on through her pores.
No one knows the secrets, fires, &
Desires that she has in store.

To them, SHE is Black.
To them, SHE is everything, even when they
Act as if SHE is nothing.

ONE WORD TO SUBDUE US ALL

Mi-nor-ity
Miniscule itty-bitty
Minor-i-tenerary
Mi-nute "it"...why?
Yours—nor my ignorance.
My-ignor-ity
Ignore the "itty-bitty" ones
whom, in your mind,
bring to thee
false glory.
4 Y must I be a MI-NOR-ITY?
I AM NOT "MINOR" OR "ITTY!"
Or is it that you simply refuse to see,
together in number,
WE are actually GREATER
than thee.

YOU MAY KNOW ME

You may know me,
But that doesn't mean you understand me.
You may truly know me...
But still, it doesn't necessarily mean that you understand me.
You may really feel like you know me,
But you still don't understand me.
And who am I?
And who am I to you?
And who are you to me?
And what is it that makes me feel
that you should understand me?
And how is it that I know that you KNOW me
but still don't understand me?
And how is it that we can agree,
if you don't understand me?
And how is it true that I can understand you
when you don't understand me?
Without an understanding between the two,
can a relationship truly be?
And if understanding was there,
would you even care, to place this relationship
where it should be?
Possibly.
It could be and would be if only you
fully understood me.
So can you relate, or can you debate
Or rate—I think my words are pretty
Straight—
Forward—so,
do you understand?

POETRY DREAMS

As the night fades into dawn,
Inside my head,
These thoughts, they carry on
In the meantime, I yawn, & yearn
For some life concepts, not yet learned.
I lay them down to sleep on my endless lawn.
I place them where they belong
Into my midnight Garden of Song
where to me, this world belongs
It won't be long,
Before this Garden of my personal psalms,
Spreads its seeds, and grows it's roots,
until these treetops split the roof,
the glass shatters, leaving the other
garden deities aloof,
bringing about the earth-shaking
awakening that allows
this vessel,
this being,
to finally seek the TRUTH!

I WILL GROW MY NAPS

I will GROW MY NAPS
If simply for the fact that
My hair JUST GROWS LIKE THAT.
But no, also because now,
My president is Black!

Because now, Mr. Corporate man,
I DARE you not to hire me because of the
TEXTURE OF MY HAIR!!!

Yet BLACK PEOPLE for decades
have walked around SCARED!!!
Afraid of their own HAIR
And wouldn't DARE be caught dead
Wit a NAPPY HEAD

I've GROWN SO WEARY OF THIS DREAD
SO WEARY of the nonsensical
History-woven thread that has bread
So much shame in our "Black hair" game!

AND when I chose to SHEAD
My straights for NAPS,
I hate
I hate
I hate that many of the sideways looks I caught
Were not from whites,
But from my fellow blacks!
But F-BOMB THAT
I'm gonna grow my NAPS anyhow.
Cause it's high time that we clued in
on the here and now!

Our hair story based on

Disgrace and confusion—
WAKE UP MY PEOPLE, it's a EFFin'
Illusion!
If your hair is Nappy like mine,
It's high time for our BLACK Hair
Evolution!
Cuz the 'Revolution' started in the 70's!
I'm sayin' let's re-gain a HAPPY NAPPY
Solution!
No more burnt, bruised scalps and breakage
From that PERM-pollution → *Perm Illusion*,
That's got YOU, my black women
Dippin' and divin', slippin' and hidin'
Under PLASTIC BAGS from the RAIN!
Just think of all the pain
You're savin' yourself…
Wasted hours spent in the salon,
self-defeating.
Defeating a most defining part of
yourself…almost beating a most
defining part of your being to DEATH.
But won't die. NAPS like Blacks,
they thrive and SURVIVE!
Black hair is an ENTERPRISE!
Although we strive to hide
Those tight, curly tendrils they,
Just like the word "Nigga" itself,
DON'T DIE!

SO I WILL GROW MY NAPS
Because to me they represent
the strength inside me, manifested
outwardly into a mane that frames
my beauty almost effortlessly.

MY NAPS: Defying Gravity.
MY NAPS: God gave them to me.
MY NAPS: of beauty.
BEHOLD US with our NAPS because our faces
Beauty can carry thee.

I WILL GROW MY NAPS, GRANDPA,
If for nothing else, for you.
For you, my predecessor, ancestors
Who denied them completely.
Out of fear, or convenience, I wear my NAPS
To BREAK A LEGACY OF SELF-HATE.
Manifested to discriminate and incriminate US
As 'lesser than' by that other man...
FEAR for me you may but Grandpa,
Need I remind you, it's a new day!
Black People, it's a great day to say:

I WILL GROW MY NAPS
To sever the illusion that "Straight-hair"
Is the only way to maintain.
It's NOT.
Don't believe the lie that justifies
Your grief, every time you look in the mirror
and see, "New Growth."
Next time instead, think:
"NO GRIEF IF I JUST LET IT GROW."
And then tell yourself in that beloved
Phrase that we now all know:
"YES WE CAN! GROW OUR NAPS!"
"YES WE WILL, GROW OUR NAPS!"
"YES, WE MUST GROW OUR NAPS!"
If we don't find them acceptable,
who else will?
And THAT will be our re-fusion, our

Re-introduction to a Nation saying:
No longer will any fiber of our beings
be repressed!
UNLEASH THEM!
UNLEASH THEM NOW ON THE REST!
And WITTNESS the days of the
Nappy News Anchor flourish!
The Nappy Executive,
The Nappy CEO of that fortune 500!
The Nappy President of the United States!
The Nappy Scientist!
The Nappy Astronaut!
Proud and Nappy citizens of the United States,
WAKE UP! And proclaim these stakes
And until you do, you all just know
That I will let MY NAPS GROW!!!

WALKS OF LIFE (SHOES WE CHOOSE)

Ah, I love 'em,
The days painted in Summertime hues.
I sit on the city bench,
People on the move...

All I can do, is watch their SHOES

Shoes.
A human means of liberating our feet from
The Earths treacherous terrain
Hot asphalt and gravel don't feel too good,
For the wandering man may travel alone,
But never without his shoes.

Sittin there, I grew bold,
Daring to ponder
The lives of the people their shoes hold...

I see
Flip-flopped suburbanites...
As their shoes beat against their soles,
They wander. Heads in the clouds,
Not a care to ponder, they are the consummate, consumer
As they blunder on in the land of urban-chaotic wonder.

Bright-sneakered urbanites...
Oh, how swiftly they walk to run
Run from the plight of life
Go on, urbanite, maintain the steady stride
Your shoes, your pride
World, step aside. urbanite stride is
Serious...wherever they end up, they're gettin'
It in their 'Jordan's' tonight!

I see
Dock martin leather sporty types...
Corporate collaborators, eating up the pavement
 in Italian-leather adornments...

I see
'Chavos' in blue and red suede gators...mmm
swag AND style....
Please allow ME to walk a mile in those shoes...hehe ;)
Perky pumps,
Sandaled flats,
Which 'walk of life' does you your shoe match?

Do your shoes say, "Obama?"
And if they did, would ya want em?!
Could YOU be proud in the shoes you walk in?

Look at your shoes...
What ARE they protecting?
Flesh and bone, heels and toes...
What HUES of yourself do you choose to expose?

WHICH have you concealed??

Don't WORRY about MY observations...
Allow me to PICK at your "Aquilles" heel...
THROW SHOES AT MY HEAD?!
Heh, well that's been done!
Try if you will...but I won't stop the questions
Until...TOGETHER...WE...HEAL.

TRANSLATION REPUDIATION

This textin this textin
This textin this textin
This textin this textin
This textin this textin
all this muther effin textin
and I STILL CAN'T SEEM
to GET M-Y P-O-I-N-T ACROSS!!!
GOD...(please) DAMN IT!!!
GOD... (please) DAMN IT ALL TO HELL!!!
PLEASE!!!
I am out of mercy for it!
My message can be as easily missed
as it can be dismissed,
and YOU STILL
probably haven't gotten the gist...!
SMH (Shaking My Head).

WHO AM I?
(AN ELEMENTAL EXHIBITION)

I am one of Gods greatest and most dangerous creations
welding the metals of first civilizations.

I am one of mankind's first God-given blessings.
Kindling the Faith of the seeker who walks with me in
    darkness...
the flickering lantern at Jobs' bedside.

Look into me and you will see,
that is IF you do not go blind...
You will see I have nothing to hide.

Put air and water aside, and for you
I will spread far and wide...
I gotta smoke a little bit before I get started,
but when I get loose,
everything else be dearly departed.

I will take life out of this world,
With wild twirls of brilliance I'll
unfurl...unleashing the hottest of heats
from my...DEEP.

BEWARE: To all that GET IN MY WAY,
for it WILL be LIFE that is to PAY!

From NOTHING does my appetite stray!

BUT
Place me in the right settings where I can manifest myself,
and get close enough to me where I can be part of your life...
and I'll provide you warmth through
all of your strife.

Embodying myself in the Sun, so it can
give the moon a face in the night...
Warming the world, and giving the sky light.
I am the producer of heat...rising. Rising from
beneath the soils to feet.
Feet to head.
Maker of desires unsaid.
I AM FIRE.

INTRODUCING...ME (THE ESSYNTIAL)

Ladies and Gentleman, I give you...

THE ESSYNTIAL

The Essyntial—in essence—meaning
Brought to you by the second college edition of the New World
Dictionary of the American Language
Meaning:
Of or constituting the INTRINSIC, FUNDAMENTAL nature of
something;
BASIC; INHERENT; ABSOLUTE;
COMPLETE; PERFECT (as she sees it)
ABSOLUTELY NECESSARY!!!
INDISPENSIBLE, REQUISITE
Containing or having the properties of, a concentrated
Abstract/extract of a plant, drug, food ect.—An Essential oil—if you will!
As was said—Something necessary of fundamental,
Indispensible, inherent of basic feature or principle—
I am, THE ESSYNTIAL...
The intrinsically fundamental
here for the purpose of jogging your mental
quintessential for your intrigue—TRUST
I am of the "other" league,
I am by no means here to mislead—indeed
I'm here to guide you—plant insight
Inside you
To provide you a glimpse of what is yet to be seen by this society.
It is part of my 'piety' that I crush
All anxieties and reciprocate what in essence,
Is known essentially only by me.
Honed by God indeed who see's me as
The Essyntial vessel for his propriety...
For God is my Proprietor and I,

A prized piece indeed.
For it is proclaimed that I alone in
His eyes am guaranteed to bloom,
Fruit, and plant seeds...
Essentially it is for me to convince you
That you too, are indeed THE ESSYNTIAL.
The essential are US the essential are WE,
And the only that can continue this
Essential legacy.
You see,

WE essentially are greatness,
and in essence,
powerful beyond imagining...BUT
Until the meek inherit this kingdom
Until we can ring in the times of true freedom,
I will be here for you all
To draw near to my words, for me
Essential for your ascension, and
US, THE ESSYNTIAL.

REDEMPTION

ON MY BAPTISM

From the wet, I rose
I felt Him—it was official.

Immediately a warm embrace,
His arms around me as I ascend from the water
my heart leaps-
landing on a cloud of SUBLIME

Inspiring a continually revolving sense of
"awe" from within me

a smile shows on the outside—true joy expresses,
but nothing can touch this most DIVINE ACCEPTANCE,
that feeling,
I want it EVERY day!

THE BREAKTHROUGH

For the longest time
I have felt the word
No.
Written on everyone's heart for me
Before a word could be spoken.

Oh, all the lies of rejection,
tattooed into my heart.

No, you're Black.
No, because you're Black.
No, because you're ugly.
No, because you don't matter.
No, because you're skinny.
No, because you're poor.
No, because you're stupid.
No, because you're different.
No. Just no.

A whale of a lie I have discovered
Inside of myself.

No, because you're weak.
No, because you're too damn strong.
No, because you're always wrong.

The no's can go on and on.

Guess what, Satan, you LOST, and YOU'RE WRONG!

I see the victory ship sailing my way, and
It's come to save me!
Easy sailing all the way,
not even a whale can stop me now.

MY ZOMBIE

Sometimes, when I'm not careful,
I can look into the mirror and see her.
My dead self.
See my zombie. She—
be my zombie.
She dead wrong,
She—
The one I gave up to be with Him, see?
Him,
the one who created me.
But she,
sometimes she comes back
Lookin' to see
if she still find herself in me.
She,
The one love fiend—
As much as she was the pusher,
she was the addict.
Selfishly in want of the lovers to love she—
Just she.
"Love me!"—said she.
"Love me and leave me the #@$% alone!"
Hell no—no
"Into-me-see" here!
You just got some booty. You should be happy.
Dead inside was her
my zombie.
Sometimes she looks at me,
Tells me how wonderful I used to be.
Cunning and stunning,
the right dress,
the right make-up,
the right attitude...

and see which man could have my gratitude tonight.
Who could possibly entertain and satisfy my appetite...
She's SUCH a monsterrrr—
Wrapped head to toe in luminous pride.
Scanning the room with lustful eyes
seeking out the biggest prize,
gluttonous for the attention of all—
The quicker she rise...
And hard will be her fall.
She just wanted it all
She just wanted everything a man could give.
Hell, she only had one life to live.
Deceitful they were in their efforts to consume her...
Diminish her magnificence
So efficiently.

Now she in the mirror
lookin' at me.
Me redeemed.
Her eyes look on...so longingly to see
into me.
Because she can't see anyone else now
but me redeemed. She
She can't see anyone else now but me redeemed.
So that zombie fade away slowly dissolved.
And left there is me,
Resolved,
and grateful for the cause
that is
Him.
He that is greater in me.

ARMED FOR LOVE

And it's too late,
God has already moved.
My heart is hardened against you.
He has carefully secured it away,
wrapped it up
Like the soft white bandages that go over hands before they are
armed with boxing mitts.
It will remain bandaged and impenetrable,
sealed by the etchings of The Word itself.
Kept.
In the safest haven this side of eternity.
Completely nestled in the cupped hands of my Heavenly Father.
He has it now.
Now If only my soul would bend a little more towards Him, too.
I can say for Him,
The cup of my soul is half full.
Please fill the rest, Lord, I am willing.
As for my mind, heh, well…
That one's a doozy.
But if anyone can reach it,
It will be God's will through me.
I will not allow my mind to subdue me.
For I am in heavy pursuit of the Truth.
I press for liberation.

Internal
External
Eternal.

MY SO CALLED ADVERSITY

Call it crack
Call it welfare
Call it "my parents just don't care"
Call it my father
Call it "Them"
Call it "they"
Call it my mother
Call it AIDS
Call it Sugar
Call it my hips
Call it my thighs
Call it the rhythm in my stride,
Call it my lips,
See it in my eyes
Call it my struggle
Call it our struggle

And this is my rebuttal to the "ADVERSITY" they place on
    me…they place on WE…UGGGGGH! ENOUGH!
Enough of trying to identify with what the world see's as Black.
So finally, we are beautiful,
Acceptable, exceptional….EQUAL.
Still…Unsatisfied.
Because the truth of EQUALITY equals
Operation "Assimilation" COMPLETE!
EVERYTHING OF OURS That remains "original"
Is now an EQUALLY optional TRADE off,
Like all cultures, now we are EQUALLY
SOLD and BOUGHT!
And BOUGHT out, traded, duplicated has been our PRIDE.
Why take pride?
Take pride.
Shove it in the nearest Antelopes "Culo"

For all I care.
I am done.
Done with that Identity game,
It had me thinking quite deranged for awhile…
My adversity.
My adversity is knowing that because I am "Black"
I MUST have been THROUGH some things…
Some things like:
No daddy syndrome.
Can't afford nothin'.
I'm a "poor nuthin" syndrome
Don't ask me nothin'
I'm deprived,
So I have an attitude, it's crude
And people are afraid of me.
I been shot at…
So now check my reality!
THIS WAS NEVER ME!!!
I have two parents and never wanted for anything—
Got put off by my own for that fact alone.
So where does a little Black one go when simply being of
   African descent doesn't cut it?
When being Black is being ghetto
Being Black is being hip-hop
Being Black is ineloquence
Being Black is blatant ignorance on display
Being Black is cool, because it always brings dismay…
That makes it good and Black..
Being Black is always fighting for being Black…
Get's tiring.
Not that I don't appreciate foundations and efforts made…
But we are so much more than descendants of freed slaves.
We aren't just freedom fighters,
We aren't just bold…
It's good to be free,

—yet we are still bought and sold
in broad daylight.
But so is every other American.
We are commodities.
So then I grab a Kufi,
Went "NAPtural"….adorned in a "new
Black." Rocked shells, instead of ice…
Wore oils and head-wraps…Rocked an ankh,
And meditated on my Beautiful "AFRIKAN SWAG!"
Felt at home there…for a while…
Forget that you don't remember…
Forget what you NEVER knew to begin with…
I am then, "BLACK AfriKAN,"
Tracing my roots will be an enterprise…
once I get there.
In the MEANTIME, I will IMPROVIZE…
And DELIGHT in the fact that I know what
These Egyptian symbols signify….SMH
Oy me!
Pssssssssh….OH PLEASE!

MY REALITY CHECK

My dear Reality gave me a check one day,
When he asked
You have sex, don't you?
I was happy to report to him that in fact...
I don't.
Not anymore. Not since I have come to know
my Lord.
Jesus.
The blood of Jesus was prayed over me one day...
after a long, unforgettable night.
The night an incubus...demon of lust
Tried to have me for life!
Cause....at one point in "mi vida"...
Masturbation.
It was more than a past time.
I named him my leisure.
Pornography,
Had me enraptured like a seizure.
It was so wild
I'd ask myself—not goin' anywhere for a while?
Let's just please her.
Because in my mind,
I was Samantha Jones, from "Sex in the City."
Falling
Into phallic fantasies
About every manor in which I could be screwed—
Watching "hot-porn.com" had my
Mind encapsulated in "prime-time bump & grind"
For hours...and hours...
And I wanted toys.
Because,
They're the safest bet—safest sex—
Well, books say, it's still none.

But that's no fun!
So they DEFINITELY
encourage masturbation.
And say that bi-curiosity is okay. Hm.
All Jesus had to say about it was to
Cut my hand off—if it causes me to stray.
Because lust is a deadly poison...
and causes much of the worlds dismay.
I wrote this to say
I am not without sin,
But praise God!
Thank you Jesus!
I am born again to WIN!
Win this fight and because of Him I no longer suffer
from sleepless nights—cause my hand just can't seem to get it right!
Or because my mind is blinded by blatant
Inhumane perversion of what sex
Is actually
Meant to be....
As dead flies give perfume a bad smell
So a little folly outweighs wisdom & honor.
Said Proverbs 10 and 1
My mind, now a tool to illuminate the Son.

Now I see,

Lust is ceaseless—Its seeds abound and
The recklessness of it all rules the life
Without... the One... who can make it all right.
Lust is not just sexual.
It unjustly deprives you of living true life.

And the reality is,
No man REALLY wants to "wife" a woman who
"Bones" as much as Samantha Jones from "Sex in the City."
Because truthfully,

This society
Places way too much 'identity' into our sex lives.
And even if I had nine lives to play with,
I would live them all for Him.
So to answer your question,
my SWEET reality is just that,
I am living the sweet, sexless life.
You want to label it?
Call me "chaste."
You want to sample this?
Call me, "Wife."

I AM SENT

Like her, I came to draw water...
Secretly in search for something more
Jesus was in front of me the WHOLE time,
Telling me what I was there for...

He called me the messenger.
To there, for Him, I was sent:
To fetch the overflowing pail,
of everlasting life.
To there, for Him, I was sent:
To bring truth and light,
to speak and deliver
the message
that is everyone's right.

To there, for Him, I was sent:
To hear the story of my wretched life...
The pain,
the strife,
what a life,
such a life,
I could not BEAR
to share alone.

To there, for Him, I was sent:
On my own, for the first time.
On my own to witness and testify.
It is not up to me to justify my own salvation!
And so to you, the nation,
I speak libations of truth.
Truth being found only through Him.

Through Him I was sent
to be the "Harvester", even though

I am no Gardener.
The harvester upon nations of fruit...
The truth unto you has now been proclaimed...
Now ripen blessed fruits,
We are Ripe.
Ripe with the promise of redemption,
Ripe with salvation...
Drinking from the wells of everlasting life!

LOVE CITADEL

I am his "Citadel."
For I WILL BE His "citadel,"
And for sure, what I am about to say
will stand alone.

You are my beloved friend, and I am
your citadel.
So when your waves of wrath come
crashing into me,
I will be strong, able to withstand your monotony.
So when I tell you that I believe everything the Word says…
That "gay" is not right, and I agree.

Don't take it personally. I love the you I see everyday.
Just not the part that claims to be "gay".

And now as you turn and walk away,
Just know that I have never walked away from you
for being gay.
And when you shout words of wrath
About me "judging", just remember the times
I've showed love to you, without budging.
And if you should go so far as to "marry" a man.
I will not love you less, but I will not be
At your wedding, I hope you'll understand
My choice.
I chose to serve God.
The one true living God, Jesus Christ.
I chose to help call out sin where it stands—
Everywhere.
Including the sin within me.
We are held accountable, us Christ followers…
Your sin, no greater than mine, see?
However your sin may lead you to blindly

obliterate me from your life.
Whereas my truth told me to love you anyway.
Sin separates. Just know that.
So as for you not to go about feeling this
to be a personal attack.
I love you, my friend, sin, none of us lack.
But sometimes it's a road to destruction,
And I'm just here to be an interruption to that.
Just know if you want to yell at me right now,
I won't yell back.
Just know that I'm here to love you.
Not to attack.
I didn't come for argument,
I came because I was asked.
I hope you can respect my difference in worldview.
I never left you, or yelled at you for being gay.
Can I get the same back for being a Christian?
I am your Citadel,
 withstanding your waves,
Always.

AREN'T YOU GLAD?

Aren't You Glad
Aren't you?
Aren't you glad I never said anything until now?
Aren't you?

Aren't you glad I never said anything
When he came for you in the night?
When he consumed all he could take
Of your essence, and goodness...when
After he was done, all that was left of you was
guilt, self-loathing and unspeakable
pride & loneliness?

Aren't you glad I never told you that
He would never stay?

Aren't you glad I never said anything
as I watched you indulge?
As you became more like the you, you want to be?
Completely senseless, and guilt free?
Free to be... under the substance influence...
Aren't you glad you don't remember what you did?
I wonder if you're glad I never told you to stop.
Were you glad when you woke up in the hospital?
Alive?
At least you're alive, right?

Aren't you glad I never told you
about Him?
Aren't you?

Now that we're all scrounging to have bread?
Now that there's just not enough oil to go around...

Now that you realize you need some…
Now that it is too late.
Do you look at me and wonder how it is
That my lamp is full and ready
For the darkness to come…

And as the darkness surrounds us,
All that you see is the light in the lantern I hold,

Aren't you glad I never told you what
Happens to those who don't have one?

Aren't you glad?

Aren't you glad that you can't see
What's there, waiting for you
in the darkness?
Aren't you?

Aren't you glad I told you this would happen?

Only,

we both never knew it would be now.

ABOUT THE AUTHOR

Cydnie Odessa is merely a vessel to the Almighty. Native to Denver Colorado, the award-winning journalist has shared her "Spoken Word" on stages with the likes of "Slam Nuba" and the Denver "Mercury Slam" teams; the city's multi-national championship winning, internationally renowned poets. The former Radio Producer of AM 670 KLTT and "Broken and Beautiful with the REAL Traci Rock" is now an advocate for "Life" and Abstinence amongst teens and young adults.

When she is not joyfully tending to the needs of others, she enjoys playing hymns and the latest pop classics on her Folk Harp.

www.ingramcontent.com/pod-product-compliance
Lightning Source LLC
Chambersburg PA
CBHW060156070426
42447CB00033B/2180